BEGINNER'S JOURNEY TO

CRYSTAL HEALING

CHARGE UP YOUR
MIND, BODY & SOUL

IAN TOWNSEND

CRYSTAL HEALING
CHARGE UP YOUR MIND, BODY & SOUL
BEGINNER'S JOURNEY

Copyright © 2016 by Ian Townsend
This document is geared towards providing exact and reliable information in regards to the topic and issue covered. The publication is sold with the idea that the publisher is not required to render accounting, officially permitted, or otherwise, qualified services. If advice is necessary, legal or professional, a practiced individual in the profession should be ordered.
From a Declaration of Principles which was accepted and approved equally by a Committee of the American Bar Association and a Committee of Publishers and Associations.
In no way is it legal to reproduce, duplicate, or transmit any part of this document in either electronic means or in printed format. Recording of this publication is strictly prohibited and any storage of this document is not allowed unless with written permission from the publisher. All rights reserved.
The information provided herein is stated to be truthful and consistent, in that any liability, in terms of inattention or otherwise, by any usage or abuse of any policies, processes, or directions contained within is the solitary and utter responsibility of the recipient reader. Under no circumstances will any legal responsibility or blame be held against the publisher for any reparation, damages, or monetary loss due to the information herein, either directly or indirectly.
Respective authors own all copyrights not held by the publisher.
The information herein is offered for informational purposes solely, and is universal as so. The presentation of the information is without contract or any type of guarantee assurance.
The trademarks that are used are without any consent, and the publication of the trademark is without permission or backing by the trademark owner. All trademarks and brands within this book are for clarifying purposes only and are the owned by the owners themselves, not affiliated with this document.

Book and Cover design by Przemyslaw Poznysz
ISBN: 978-1542393812
First Edition: December 2016

CONTENTS

INTRODUCTION 5

CHAPTER 1.
CRYSTALS AND STONES TO GET STARTED WITH 7

CHAPTER 2.
INTRODUCTION TO CHAKRAS 17

CHAPTER 3.
CONNECTIONS BETWEEN CRYSTALS & CHAKRAS 23

CHAPTER 4.
PREPARING CRYSTALS FOR USE 27

CHAPTER 5.
MAINTENANCE OF YOUR CRYSTALS 33

CHAPTER 6.
EFFECTS BOTH MENTAL AND PHYSICAL.................... 37

CONCLUSION 47

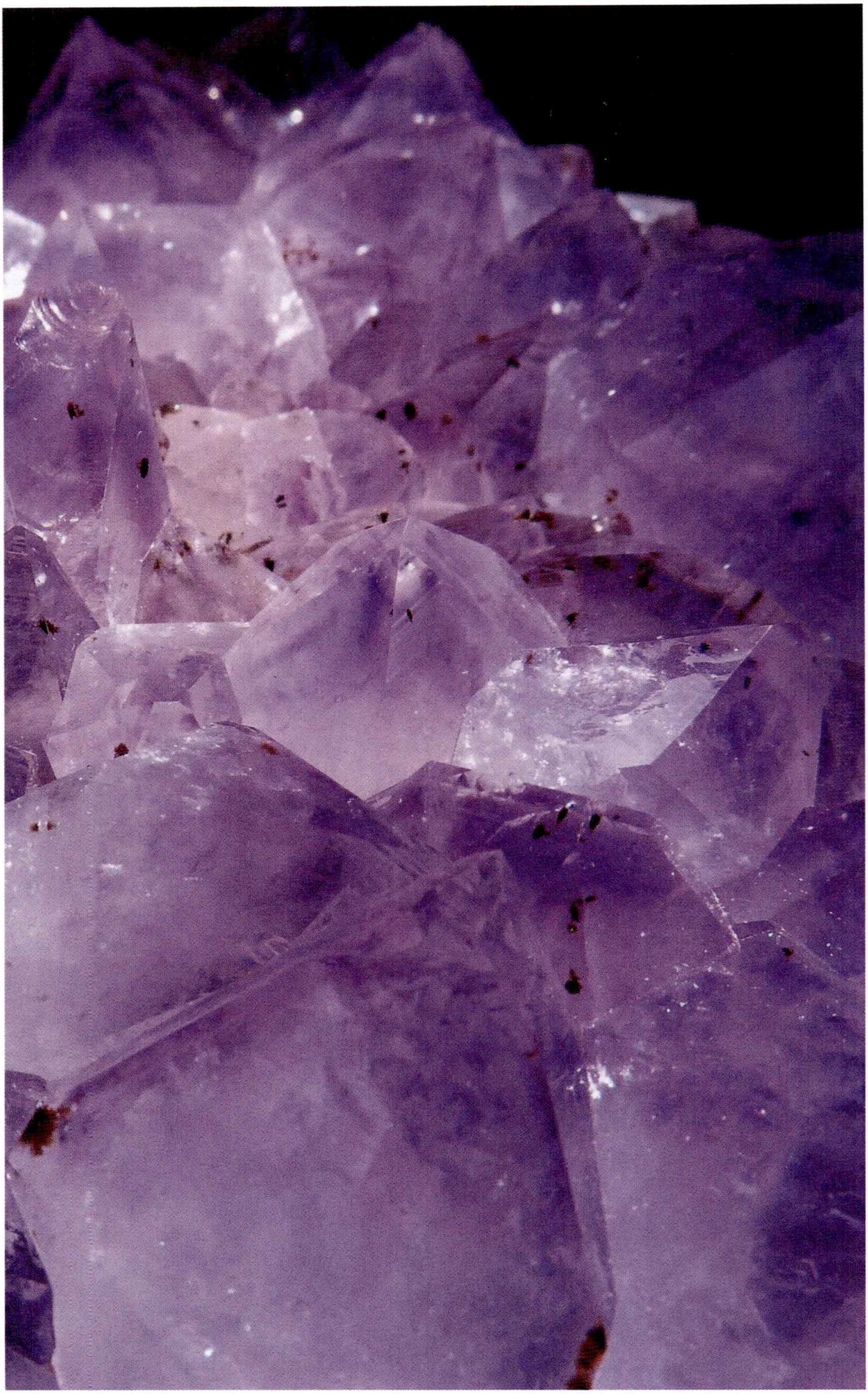

INTRODUCTION

These special stones aren't simply just for looks, although they are very pleasing to the eye. Crystals all contain various charges and functions that border on powers of the divine, with both mental and physical effects that are equally daunting. Through this book, you'll learn the proper care, treatment, and use of crystals to fit any situation you choose!

Crystal healing, historically, had been used for centuries in many different kinds of ancient cultures. However, crystals have seen a continuing spike in popularity since the very beginning of the twenty-first century. Whether this is because of rising prices of common medicine fostering a search for a better way of healing, or simply because of the recent interest in the crystals themselves, their popularity has swept across nations as methods of healing and therapy. Many say this is for good reason, that each crystal contains links to the emotions or energies moving throughout the body.

This book will hopefully have given some insight on the usage and proper care of these special stones, and an accurate description of their effects. With this book, you will gain new knowledge of how and why they work, and their connections to seven energy centers called chakras. Once you discover their various uses, you'll be keeping a rock of Hematite or Aquamarine with you wherever you go. Thank you again for downloading this book, I hope you'll enjoy it!

CHAPTER 1. CRYSTALS AND STONES TO GET STARTED WITH

The different kinds of special stones, all containing various properties and connotations, have been lumped under the common name of "crystals." Their colors can range from a pure translucent white to a dark red or blue. Most are crystalline and have multiple sides, are hard, and reflect light, though some look like simple rocks of different shapes and sizes.

Size of crystals generally determines the amount of energy it can hold, as well as if there are any smudges or cracks in the crystal. When looking for the size of the preferred crystal, one might first examine what its use will likely be; is it used for helping to sleep, or to help with work? Is it used to help ground yourself, or protect your home from negative energy? If the stone is being used for things that can be done while stationary, it is wise to keep the crystal in a set location. If not, and it is used more often and for more various tasks, keep the crystal close, preferably on a pendant, bracelet, or simply in a pocket.

There are hundreds of different types of crystals with varying colors, degrees of hardness, and properties. It would take far too much time to describe all, or even most of the crystals that exist. However, the chief crystals mainly associated with different shades and colors (Aquamarine, Garnet, Amethyst, and Sapphire) are easily catalogued and described. These are a few of the more common stones you can find to get started with.

AMETHYST

Amethyst is a valuable crystal that ranges from dark to light purple in hue. It is actually one of the few varieties of quartz that exist, and has a few "brothers" that share this distinction. Amethyst is a symbol of strength and self-control, said to bring many kinds of wealth and a clear head. It can also be a good protection stone, as it's often used to repel negative energy.

Amethyst is great to help with physical conditions and emotional issues. Its healing powers are mainly used to cure ailments of the nervous system, especially of nightmares and insomnia. It is very calming and soothing feeling while meditating with this crystal.

Amethyst supports our mind, it reduces anxieties that are followed up by headaches and migraines. Hold it when getting stressed, angry or tough situation is just too overwhelming

AGATE

Agate is a stone that looks as if it has several rings surrounding a usually smooth surface of brown. Agate is a potent stone used for healing and protection, and are often used for amulets.

This crystal is beneficial to the heart and blood vessels. Just wear it on a pendant in the middle chest area, aiding the cardiac muscle.

Agate improves operation of our mind, boosts concentration and analytical thinking. It heals emotional disharmony and can be useful for any kind of trauma.

AVENTURINE

Aventurine is a stone ranging from light to very dark green in hue. Its domains range from luck in finding love to the achievement of dreams. The stone is meant to promote harmony.

It is especially supportive to people with circulatory issues and is fantastic while recovering from surgery. It may aid in lowering cholesterol and preventing heart attacks.

Aventurine's energy balances and harmonizes emotions. It soothes emotional wounds, calms irritation and anger. It stimulates a sense of hope and joy.

BLOODSTONE

Bloodstone is a very powerful healing stone, looking like plain, smooth, metal stones of darker colors. Bloodstone is used to detox and cleanse the body and mind, and is also a popular stone for strength and energy.

It improves immune system, eliminating toxins from the body and purifying the blood. It has been used to alleviate lower back pain and to soothe mosquito bites.

Bloodstone's powerful energy enhances strength and courage. If the illness can't be cured and there is a need to face the reality of death and human mortality, bloodstone helps to move forward in those times.

CLEAR QUARTZ

Clear quartz is a stone that is generally translucent in appearance, without many impurities. Quartz is often associated with helping energy to flow more smoothly throughout the body, and for obtaining mental clarity.

It is considered as a master crystal, and can be used for any physical condition. It treats motion sickness or dizziness. If used in a form of an elixir, it eliminates all kinds of toxins from the body, and helps with problems in the digestive system.

Clear quartz enhances positive thoughts and clears the mind from any negativity. It provides clarity in thinking and improves awareness, gives a better view on some of the most common problems people face every day.

GARNET

Photo by Géry Parent

Garnet is usually a dark red stone that sometimes is translucent. It is often associated with helping energy flow, creating joy, and helping deal with depression while promoting physical activity.

It improves body regeneration, purifies the blood and treats spinal disorders. Garnet helps with assimilating vitamins and minerals into the system.

It is very useful in times of crisis, in those situations garnet strengthens the mind, bringing great courage. Kept under a pillow, it is thought to alleviate nightmares.

HEMATITE

Hematite is a smooth, hard stone that ranges from silvery gray to dark gray in hue. It is used to help keep the body balanced and to assist with breathing deeply. Hematite is known as an excellent grounding stone.

It aids in blood conditions, enhances and regulates supply of the blood in the body. Helps with assimilation of iron and creation of blood cells. Treats cramps and assist with healing fractures.

Hematite is a very strong crystal for supporting the mind. It enhances willpower, survivability and boosts confidence. It aids in overcoming all kind of addictions and compulsive behaviors.

JADE

Jade is another smooth, hard stone that is usually a lighter green or a sea-green. Jade has a huge significance in many Asian cultures. Jade has been used to motivate achieving dreams, and helps foster long lifetimes.

It is one of the most powerful cleansing stones, perfect for kidney issues. It removes toxins and balances the body fluids alkaline ratios.

Jade soothes the mind, keeping your thoughts out of any negativity. It boosts confidence, and it helps to find the courage in very humiliating circumstances.

LAPIS LAZULI

Photo by Géry Parent

Often shortened to Lapis, Lapis Lazuli is usually a deep blue in color, and rather smooth. Lapis Lazuli is one of the oldest stones on the planet, some saying it was there from Earth's very beginning. Lapis helps to foster the Throat Chakra (see in chapters 2 and 3), and helps with sight and negative energy.

It alleviates hearing issues and other ear and nasal complications. After a good soak in sunlight, lowers bruising and aids in skin conditions.

Lapis Lazuli gives a better awareness of beliefs, and clearer mind of entirety of life. Unveils emotional limitations and at the same time shows opportunities to enhance abilities.

MALACHITE

Photo by Géry Parent

    Malachite is a green and black smooth stone, the green usually taking the form of large, wide rings on black surface. Malachite is used for purification and is often sought after as a stone to help cope with negativity.

    It regulates the menstrual cycle and cramps. It resonates especially strong with female organs, treats all kind of sexual diseases. It is well known to lower blood pressure, successful in treating epilepsy and travel sickness.

    Malachite encourages any positive, emotional change. Alleviates shyness and inspires to express strong feelings. It helps with fighting against depression and finding the strength within to overcome fears.

CRYSTAL HEALING

OBSIDIAN

Obsidian is a smooth, black glass-like stone often found around active and inactive volcanoes alike. Obsidian helps to control dark impulses like fear, and is used as a significantly powerful grounding stone.

It is used as a stone of protection, repelling all the emotional negativity. It helps to move on after tough breakups. Hold obsidian for a moment just above the Third Eye (this Chakra is located over eyebrows, read chapter 2) and it will break through any mental barrier.

PERIDOT

Peridot is a smooth, unclear stone that ranges from light yellow to lightish green in color. It is often used as a stone to help the transfer of energy through the body, and is seen as a symbol of happiness and purity.

It balances the endocrine system, which conduct the health of the physical body, and helps to vitalize the entire system, making it stronger and healthier. It aids digestion, making vitamins and minerals from food and water easier to assimilate.

Peridot is a great stone to heal emotional side of the body, cleansing and lessening anger, jealousy, while cultivating one to understand importance of holding onto people.

CRYSTAL HEALING

ROSE QUARTZ

Photo by Géry Parent

    Rose Quartz is, indicated from the title, a generally smooth stone ranging from pink to a very light purple in hue. Rose Quartz is used to help mitigate stress and alleviate tension, and is a useful symbol of love.

    If applied as an elixir, it can help to clear any impurities on the skin, reducing wrinkles. It may also aid in lowering the appearance of scars. Rose Quartz is great for people that went through physical heart issues, skipped beats, irregular heart rhythm.

    Rose Quartz's beautiful pink hue emanations, soothes and heals the biggest wounds the heart has suffered, aiding in ability to give and receive love. It disperses sorrows, fears and worries.

SMOKY QUARTZ

Photo by Géry Parent - Smoky Quartz and Garnet

Smoky Quartz is a smooth, often reflective stone that is brown to light gray in hue. It is a useful grounding stone and a good stone for controlling emotions and tensions throughout the body.

It has healing abilities to cure bad effects of radiation, like sunburn, or longer exposure to radioactive materials. It has been used to relieve muscle cramps and headaches.

Smoky Quartz alleviate fear and stress, lifting our soul to fight with depression. Teaches to let go of negative feelings, what is no longer helping with personal growth. It creates great power to change reality and manifest dreams.

TIGER'S EYE

Tiger's Eye is a very commonly known smooth stone, with many brown stripes varying in size. Tiger's eye is a useful stone for optimistic thought and is also often utilized for most kinds of healing.

It is used to boost vitality and strength, bringing body balance on all possible levels. Placed around intimate area, it can stimulate fertility and alleviate issues from past experiences.

Tiger's Eye is an enormous ally of emotions and the mind, balancing extremes and helps dispersed thoughts to come together in a way that they make sense.

Again, these are a stark few of the precious and semi-precious minerals that have these properties. Many different names for the stones described exist, as well as for the others not listed. These stones are by no means the only ones to look for.

Of these stones, Quartz is the greatest in number, as there are many different varieties of it. On top of this, Quartz makes up about one eighth of the Earth's crust, which is around 3.5 quintillion tons of mineral. Quartz comes in many different shapes and colors, with lots of different colorations linked to the impurities it has. Most common Quartz is white and/or translucent, and has multiple flat sides and edges.

A few of these stones are associated with months of the year, such as Emerald being for May and Garnet for January. These different "birthstones" would also have something of a personal connection to the user, due to their association with the very day they were born. This translates to it being a good idea to hold an Emerald on your person if you were born in May.

Some stones are crystalline, and some are not, and others still look like simple rocks or metals. Hematite is a smooth, silvery-gray and black stone, but not necessarily a crystal, though its properties as a grounding stone are magnificent. The same goes for Jade, as it is typically a smooth green stone, though not necessarily a crystal.

These are many of the more commonly found stones sought after in different shops and marketplaces. A lot of them are iconic for several reasons; some of them are birthstones (Peridot, Emerald, Garnet), and still more have colors named after them. These stones are considered essential to have for their ease of access to collecting them, their widespread and versatile uses.

CHAPTER 2.
INTRODUCTION TO CHAKRAS

The Chakras are an anomalous form of explaining energies flowing through the bodies, and their various attributes to the personalities of different people. The thought and study of these Chakras spreads back to ancient Indian thought; indeed, the word 'Chakra' means 'wheel of spinning energy.' The school of thought around chakras has spread to several different Far Eastern cultures for millennia. In fact, they've made several different appearances in various forms of pop culture as well.

Many do not know all, if not any, of the chakras, and those that do study them passively know of only seven. In actuality, there are over a hundred different chakras, however the seven Chakras are the most commonly known and studied around the world, and many cultures say all of the 114 Chakras are rooted to seven main ones.

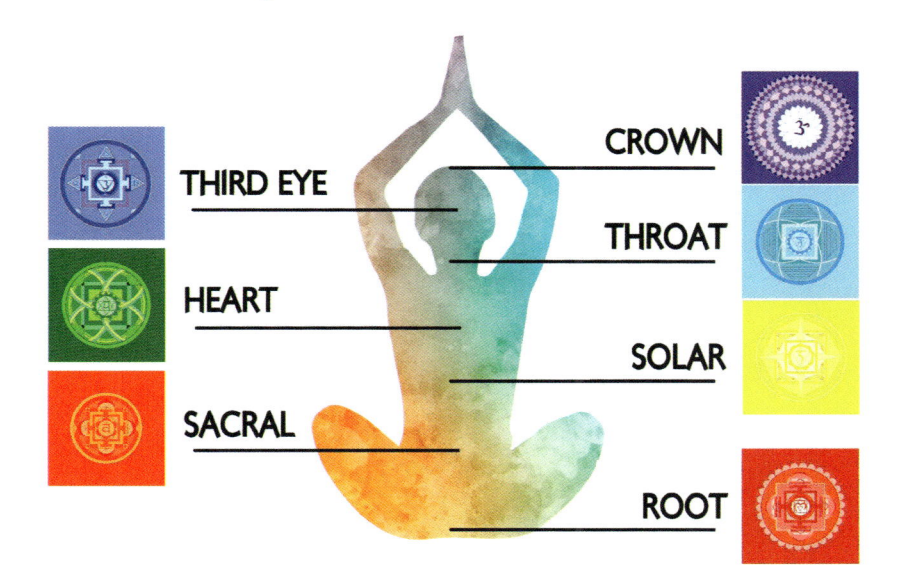

Major seven Chakras are, from top to bottom: Crown, Third Eye, Throat, Heart, Solar, Sacral, and Root. Each of them is placed in a center line going upwards from the bottom of the spine to the very top of the head. The Chakras all have different meanings and uses for interpretation, and personality traits in certain people are often indicators for the chakras they use the most. For example, if you were an effective communicator or extroverted, you would have a strong Throat Chakra. Each Chakra governs a different set of domains.

ROOT

The Root Chakra is located at the lowest tip of the backbone. This Chakra is the one most mentioned in terms of grounding oneself, and is heavily connected to the lower body in general. When this Chakra is weakened, or "blocked," fear and procrastination may come about.

Those with good instincts and calm, collected heads usually have a strong Root Chakra. People with talent for business and management have a strong connection to their Root Chakra.

SACRAL

The Sacral Chakra, also called the Navel Chakra, is located at the very center of the stomach. It is mostly representative of the organs involved with blood, as well as the kidneys and liver. The Sacral Chakra also governs over most aspects of feeling and emotion, and is often connected to sexual desire. When this Chakra is blocked, there is much emotional turmoil, withdrawal, and obsession.

Those with clear, controlled emotions and a lack of negativity have a strong Sacral Chakra. Many different singers and actors have strong Sacral Chakras, for their impressive ability to reach into emotional reservoirs.

SOLAR

The Solar Chakra is located in the Solar Plexus, one of the few muscles our body has a considerably hard time trying to flex. It mostly represents the digestive system and muscles, and is connected to the Sacral Chakra in that it also controls emotions. Blockage may result in being flustered and irritated often.

Those that are cheerful and free of negativity have a strong Solar Chakra. Great athletes have good Solar Chakras for their connection to the muscles.

HEART

The Heart Chakra is located at the very center of the breast, directly in between the upper part of the ribcage. Unsurprisingly, the Heart Chakra is also connected to the circulatory system, and regulates feelings of infatuation and unconditional love. However, the Heart Chakra is also responsible for even, deep breathing, and is constantly in flux with other emotional Chakras. Blockage of this Chakra may result in feelings of abandonment or helplessness.

Those with a strong Heart Chakra are driven and very guided emotionally, choosing to "listen to their heart," so to speak. Lovers, songwriters, and poets would have exceptionally good Heart Chakras.

THROAT

The Throat Chakra is located at the neck, just above the collarbone. The Throat Chakra is connected to the hands, shoulders, and vocal cords, and is in control of most oratory functions and methods of communication. Speaking, singing, and most other kinds of creative expression are rooted to this Chakra. Blockage of the Throat Chakra leads to stuttering, mumbling, and lack of creativity.

Those with strong Throat Chakras have excellent judgement, are immensely creative, and effective at speaking and communicating. Orators, speechwriters, and lawyers have good Throat Chakras.

THIRD EYE

The Third Eye Chakra is located around the forehead, often painted to be just above the eyebrows or between them. This Chakra is associated with the brain, nose, ears, mouth, and as such covers the domain of the five senses. The Third Eye also controls many kinds of rational thought, and is connected with inquisitive behavior. A blocked Third Eye Chakra leads to closed-mindedness, a lack of foresight, and idleness of thought.

Those with strong Third Eyes are considered very wise and skeptical. Mathematicians, event planners, and scientists have exceptionally good Third Eye Chakras.

CROWN

The Crown Chakra (as the name would suggest) is labeled at the very top of one's head. Physically, it works in conjunction with the Third Eye with the brain, and also indicates control of the nervous system. This Chakra is connected to knowledge, intelligence, and rational thought. Where this differs with the Third Eye is often unclear, but many make the distinction of the Third Eye being what we perceive, and the Crown to be with what we believe. Those with blocked Crown Chakras are known to have poor mental health, and is often associated with diseases like schizophrenia, Alzheimer's, addiction and common headaches.

Those with a strong Crown Chakra are able to process information relatively easily, and are very attuned spiritual thinkers. Clergymen and philosophers have excellent Crown Chakras.

The Chakras also have different colors associated with them, with the Root being red, the Sacral being orange, the Solar being yellow (again, not surprising), the Heart being green, the Throat being blue, the Third Eye being indigo, and the Crown being a deeper purple. Some of the distinctions between the Chakras are very blurred lines, seeing as how the domains can sometimes overlap. Nonetheless, each Chakra has its own, specific domains that are specific to it.

Where this fits in with the stones mentioned earlier is rather simple. Some stones strengthen, or "open" Chakras, and others help the flow of energy to these Chakras, and thus throughout the body. Others still may help to even out the flow of energy from the Chakras, maintaining balance and stability with energy input and output. Some of their connections are described in Chapter 3.

CHAPTER 3. CONNECTIONS BETWEEN CRYSTALS & CHAKRAS

Obsidian is a good example of a powerful stone for grounding, which is directly connected to the Root Chakra. Citrine is meant to repel negative energy and is associated with Solar Chakra. Loads of crystals and stones are connected to specific Chakras, and others inspire emotions like love, and states of mind, for example creativity.

Below is a list of Chakras and stones connected with them. Later on I'll tell a bit about stones that are associated with the flow of energy.

Root: Hematite, Black Obsidian, Garnet, and Smoky Quartz are often connected to the root chakra. They're generally used as grounding stones for keeping your body centered and on its foundation.

Sacral: Turquoise, Fluorite, and Copper are largely associated with the Chakra placed at the naval. They're used for strengthening emotional stability and acceptance.

Solar: Amber, Tiger's Eye, and Citrine are meant to amplify the Solar Chakra, and are useful for supporting confidence and self-esteem.

Heart: Rose Quartz, Aventurine, and Malachite are stones connected with the Heart Chakra, and are used for strengthening feelings of love and passion.

Throat: Aquamarine, Amazonite, and Celestite are heavily linked to the Throat Chakra, and help to foster clear communication and strong, fair judgements.

Third Eye: Surprisingly few stones are commonly connected to the Third Eye Chakra, the most popular ones that has been discovered are Azurite and Lapis Lazuli. These stones help to support the ability to focus and thinking with clarity.

Crown: Topaz, Amethyst, and Selenite are commonly associated with the Crown Chakra. When used properly, these stones can help with spirituality and contentedness.

Several more stones are used for the transportation of energy throughout the body as well, such as calcite and citrine. Others help to create different, more positive emotions; rose quartz and black tourmaline are commonly sought after for this purpose, and stones connected to the Sacral, Solar, and Heart Chakras all have some success from their general connection to the Chakras that foster emotional response.

Clear quartz is said to be masterful at healing physical and mental debilitations. Amethyst is widely renowned for the multitude of purposes it has in almost all areas of the body and mind. Several more of these special stones exist for different purposes and attributes and deserve consideration for their uses.

CHAPTER 4. PREPARING CRYSTALS FOR USE

The use of crystals is not as clear cut as wearing them around your neck, or hanging them similar in fashion to a dream catcher. Many of the special stones require different kinds of preparation and planned uses to utilize them effectively. The need for these methods of preparation are all but necessary for the crystals to be productive for any kind of use.

Many of the methods of preparation described below are rather simple. Not a lot of extra products are needed to prepare the crystals for use, and many different methods require things that can be found very easily. While the task of preparing them may seem mundane or tedious, it is needed in order for the stones to live out their usefulness. Described below are a few ways of preparing the crystals, discharging them of negative energy, and purifying them.

CLEANSING

Cleansing crystals before and after use keeps them free of any blockage, their potential easily accessed, and of course keeping them clean and aesthetically pleasing. There are dozens of different known effective methods of cleansing crystals, most of which are relatively easy to do. The methods described work for most (if not all) crystals on the market to this day.

Water is the simplest instrument of cleansing a crystal, because of its astounding and symbolic quality to wash the impurities, and to rid it of the stored energy that would murk it. Running water from any kind of sink would suffice naturally, though water rich in minerals, such as streams and rivers, are considered extremely useful for keeping the crystals at maximum productivity. Simply hold the crystal in the stream of water, or place it down and let it sit, and rub it dry with a clean cloth.

Different minerals can help to cleanse crystals as well, and placing the crystal on or near the chosen mineral is generally highly successful. Allow the crystal to sit in place with the mineral of choice, a few of the more common choices being iron or iodine, and stay for a few minutes. Any other mineral that is a known energizer will suffice for this task.

Even simpler methods exist, as many are known to hold their crystal under the moon for an entire night, and have it cleansed the next morning. Alternatively, you can let it sit in the sun to have it burn away the impure energy contained within. Either method tends to be just as effective, though full moons are known to work particularly well for cleansing.

Holding the crystal under bright yellow or white light for prolonged periods are slow, yet ample methods for cleaning them as well. Be advised: make sure to place the crystals so that the rays from the light do not pose a fire hazard. Any crystal that reflects light can have it magnify light that could start a fire. This also applies for the aforementioned sun-cleansing method.

Using sea salt or any other kind of salt is a hit-and-miss deal for quite a few crystals. Many crystals can be eroded by salts, or they can block the crystal's output altogether. Salt should generally be avoided when working with crystals, regardless of type.

Many different flower petals contain the ability to cleanse crystals as well. Soaking the petals of roses or chrysanthemums in water, and then placing the crystals in the bowl with the petals can cleanse the crystals if let be for a few hours. Gently rub down the crystal with a cloth when finished.

CHARGING

Charging the crystal is used to allow it to store and put out energy more efficiently. It allows for the output and input of energy to be honed and clear, and to allow the crystal to run at peak efficiency. Charging crystals is essential for their preparation for use, as charging them will let them live up their uses.

Charging is different from cleansing through a specific borderline between the terms themselves. Cleansing is filtering out the energy from the crystal, effectively starting out with a blank slate after the crystal has absorbed, and subsequently discharged, negative energy. Charging fills the crystal with positive energy once more, making it more effective within its means of use. Both are essential to helping crystals function without hindrance.

Overall, sun remains the most common and effective method of charging crystals. Considering that sun bristles with energy itself, it is no wonder that it would transfer over to the crystal that it fills. Cleansing and charging the crystal can be effectively done in one fell swoop by using sun rays and moon, letting it sit out for a full day will have likely satisfied both purposes. Result after charging crystals is higher concentration of positive energy in them, keeping all properties at their peaks.

PROGRAMMING

Programming the crystal provides it with a more personal touch as to its owner's needs and wants for the crystal's purposes. Essentially, programming is much like imprinting oneself onto the crystal, to allow the crystal to become more effective to their user.

One method of programming is to take the crystal, holding in both hands, stare at it, and think of what you wish the crystal to help you with. It sounds simple at first, but human thoughts require a surprising amount of focus to transmit them to even the smallest or most potent of crystals. Crystals are extremely receptive, but only if the energy is present to be stored and used.

Another method is to hold the crystal, gently rub it, and ask the crystal out loud what you want it to achieve. It seems rather silly to think about doing, but still remains as a viable method of imprinting onto the crystal. Keep in mind, what one asks of the crystal must be realistic and simple to do at first, in order for the message to come across with accuracy. The key is to focus on the words you're asking, and to convey them with the deepest of meaning; do not mumble or hesitate on the words.

Programming the crystal is much like making a computer program, except much simpler. It essentially encodes the crystal with the user's psyche and user preferences. Just as the code can be written, it can be wiped away as well. Simply overwrite the crystal with the current owner's desires, if it had a previous owner.

In none of the preparation steps listed should hot water be used. Hot water can damage the crystal's structure and weaken it. Avoid any kind of plastic being around the crystal as much as possible. Otherwise, these steps should be constantly repeated to keep one's crystal functioning properly and efficiently.

CHAPTER 5. MAINTENANCE OF YOUR CRYSTALS

The needs of keeping energy within crystals clean and the crystal itself productive is expressed profusely throughout the populous that supports it. However, in order for the crystal to work, be it filled with any kind of energy or none at all, it needs to remain physically intact. Below are a few things to note about making sure your crystals are not damaged, defaced, or destroyed.

The majority of keeping crystals stored is common sense. Much like glass, any fragile crystals must be kept safe from obstructions, and should preferably be kept in a closed container to deter breaking. Small crystals should be kept in closed containers as well; you don't want to lose them. Harder or bigger crystals should be kept away from pets and very young children, and from large heights, for fear of choking hazards and pain it may cause falling on somebody. A good method of keeping your crystals stored somewhere, especially if moving, is to keep the crystals in an easily identifiable container that one can access with ease. No matter the circumstance, keeping your crystals close at hand is crucial to their usefulness in different situations. Elaborate boxes are usually not needed, as small fabric bags or a marked box would suffice for keeping them within reach.

Keep crystals away from dry areas and exposure to any kind of mildew. When staying in one location, glass cases for holding crystals are excellent ideas, and are perfect for making displays with them as well. Furthermore, keeping your crystals within reach of light fixtures will allow them to be both easily seen and well displayed. Glass cases and small, elaborate metal boxes are great places to store crystals if staying in a stationary location.

Physically cleaning crystals can be a bit of a struggle, depending on the crystals. Sometimes, crystals are unable to be cleaned by most conventional methods, as they can be too brittle to work into properly. Harder crystals like Quartz and Diamond are easier to deal with, as a clean cloth and some elbow grease can usually clean out the spots. If the spots are harder to go after, all-purpose cleaner will generally not affect your crystal negatively.

The issue with "softer" crystals is that they can break or even fall apart if not given the proper care. Do not use any kinds of rough, scratching surfaces on or around crystals. The best bet is to use a soft cloth dipped in water, and to have the crystal carefully rubbed with delicacy until shining again.

Polishing crystals, much like cleaning them with water and a cloth, can also be a bit tricky. Many use a flame polish technique, which involves running a hot flame slowly across a crystal. This should only be used for harder crystals; as softer ones can break apart as they expand with heat. For most kinds of polishing, soak the crystals in vinegar or ammonium cleaner, and apply a soft cloth to wipe away any smudges to allow the crystal to shine. However, keep track of the crystal itself, and read up on it to make sure it won't react harmfully to any of the chemicals.

Any crystal with multiple hard sides and edges should be kept away from hot water. If the crystal is put in hot water, it could very easily crack. When cleansing the crystal, keep them out of hot water and run them through cold water instead. If the crystal cracks, it loses aesthetic quality, and often loses some of its power as well.

The hardness of crystals, before creation of the famed Mohs Hardness Scale, was a bit of a daunting issue. However, thanks to Mohs, identifying and arranging crystals based on their specific hardness is key to being able to shop them and keep them clean. Again, Quartz, Diamond, and Garnet are considered very hard, whereas Talc, Calcite and Fluorite are considered soft.

Most of the time, the hardness of crystals can be deduced quite easily by ourselves; if it's crystalline and heavy, it's most likely pretty hard. Likewise, the same can be said for crystals that look shiny and brittle, that they're likely classified as "soft." For more detailed examination, or simply just for reassurance that you're doing the right thing for the crystal, refer to the Hardness Scale.

CHAPTER 6. EFFECTS BOTH MENTAL AND PHYSICAL

As explained before, crystals have a variety of uses, many attributed to the physical and mental form. Below are some of those uses, and how to properly apply to them.

INJURY

Towards physical healing, it is a very crucial fact to note that crystals are not engines of which to create miracles. For instance, if a user were to fall down a cliff and have their leg broken, a crystal would not magically repair it. Granted, it may dull the pain a bit and relieve some of the weariness from blood loss, but this indirect support is not to be confused with repairing of physical damage. While crystals are helpful, do not expect them to magically cure you.

However, as stated, crystals do have effects towards alleviating physical pain caused by said damage. Some crystals are known to ease pain and to aid blood loss to some degree; quartz is a large example of this, being one of the greatest healing crystals known to man. Opal is useful for many different bone-related injuries. Black Pyrite is excellent for treating infections caused by these wounds.

To be completely clear, this is not advice to skip going to the doctor or the ER if something is wrong. Rubbing crystals on the affected area is a poor substitute for having your shoulder popped into place by a practitioner. However, crystals do serve some use for physical injury. Simply rub the cleansed crystal on or near the injured area, and breathe deeply and evenly to allow the crystal to work.

OTHER PHYSICAL PROBLEMS

This is a bit of an umbrella term; many different uses for crystals fit inside of the body rather than out as is. However, the uses for crystals and the internal ailments they can help to fix are extremely numerous. Generally, crystals can relieve all kinds of problems happening within the body, of course within reason. Be warned, the stone must be cleansed and programmed to treat the ailment, and the stone should be compatible with helping to treat the affliction.

Headaches, be they caused by sinuses, pressure, or pure stress of an overworked mind, are easily curable by crystals. Blue Sapphire and Purple Agate work especially well for this task, and are able to relieve pressure from the brain rather well. Simply press the crystal to your forehead, relax the muscles, and breathe deeply. Energy from the crystal should flow into your body rather quickly.

Digestion is a crucial (yet entirely too susceptible) part of the human body. The digestive system is one of the most extensive, though there are quite a few stones that can alleviate it. Opal and Amber are very helpful with problems of this matter, and any crystal associated with the Sacral and Solar Chakras also serve some use. Run the crystal along your stomach and lower chest, while lying back to keep the digestive tract flat. The crystal should help the pain within minutes.

Back pain, locked joints, bad knees and aching shoulders are usually related to issues in the bones. Several crystals seem almost designed to help with this problem, Black Opal and Green Quartz being two that stand out above the rest. Rub the crystal along the aching area while breathing evenly. The crystal will have a rather underwhelming effect compared to the other illnesses to be healed, considering the amount of sinew between the crystal and the bone, so the effect will be gradual and mitigated; daily application and cleansing is advised.

Breathing problems have become a recently rampant problem in human history; smoking becoming a huge issue, smog levels recently spiking, and just how vulnerable the respiratory system is, these are immense factors that hinder breathing. Crystals like Pink Opal and Black Quartz help to heal the lungs and alleviate breathing problems through constant application, as well as stones connected to the throat Chakra. Simply rub from the back and front upwards to the throat to just under the chin, and breathe as deeply as possible. Be advised: this is not a substitute for a blocked airway. If someone is physically unable to breathe because they're choking from an allergic reaction or otherwise, contact emergency medical personnel immediately.

Heart disease and problems related to it are another increasing problem, especially in the United States. Blood pressure and sugar problems are rampant in most developed countries, though there are crystals able to help problems with the heart. Any Heart Chakra-related crystals, Emerald and Peridot are widely useful for helping heart problems. Hold the crystal close to your heart, and run it along visible veins, making sure you are in a relaxed position. Problems like heartburn and hypertension should go down relatively quickly, though helping problems like blood sugar and pressure will take much more exposure.

Kidneys are responsible for majority of the excretory system, as they filter blood and other fluids to create urine. As such, they are extremely crucial to keeping the body in optimum condition, and running into problems relating to them can create problems for the entire body. Crystals like Celestite and Topaz can help to filtrate fluids and with passing of kidney stones. Hold the crystal just under the ribcage, taking shallow and even breaths. Depending on the issue, it could take minutes to hours to see noticeable progress.

Some of us have motivation to do things, such as go to the gym or work, but simply lack the energy to keep up. Some stones, like those connected to the Sacral Chakra, and others like Carnelian and Malachite, are monumentally helpful for opening up new reservoirs of energy. Keep one with you during strenuous activity, or keep one at your bedside as you wake up for both better mood and energy for the day.

Most of the methods of curing ailments have to do with holding or rubbing the crystal onto the afflicted area. If not, simply meditating with them is a safe method of curing. For physical debilitations, stones have a gradual and somewhat diluted effect compared to mental effects.

MENTAL EFFECTS

Crystals have a much stronger association with spiritual energy and mentalities than with the physical body. Granted, the Chakras are linked to different parts of the body, and most crystals are associated with the Chakras, but the connection of the crystals to the body is thus only by extension; crystals are able to affect the mind and moods more directly than they can the body. This does not mean that crystals don't have considerable effects on the physical form, but that they generally have a faster and stronger connection to the mind.

Stress is a natural part of daily life, to many. Stress is a useful catalyst for us to get things done, though it is easily able to overwhelm us with it. Luckily, several stones can be programmed and used for the purpose of dispelling the stress. Albite and Purple Jade are ample healers of stress, and are known to treat it fairly well. Simply relax, and meditate anywhere from a few minutes to an hour and a half, with a cleansed crystal on your person. The energy will begin to work smoothly, so long as your mind is able to be cleared, and the room is free from distractions.

Addiction is a troubling and thoroughly daunting mental and physiological problem sweeping the world from the beginning of humans seeking any kind of vice. Addiction is described as being dependent or reliant on a certain substance or feeling to get through the day, and is not limited to narcotics; caffeine and natural adrenaline are some examples of these. However, there are a few stones useful for helping face the problems of addiction, Azurite and Carnelian being two of them. Crystals associated with the Sacral Chakra are also useful for caffeine addiction. Meditate with them close at hand and clear of negative energy, and feelings or pangs of need may become dulled after several minutes.

Depression is a psychological and physiological condition that has multitudes of prescription and over-the-counter medication to treat it. However, if you look at the side effects for said medications, it can almost seem to do more harm than good. Several stones are known to help raise spirits from depressive thoughts and actions, Smoky Quartz and Lapis being two common ones. You might also try stones linked to the Root and Heart Chakra. Hold them close and meditate with them, or wear a cleansed stone around your neck or wrist, and much of the negative energy can start to slip away. However, depression is a complex anomaly, and it could be weeks for much progress to show.

Grief affects most, if not all people, and is linked to emotional distress and depression. The famous "Five Stages of Grief" can have daunting effects, but there are several stones to help combat those same effects. Rose Quartz and Selenite can help to aid with the passing of a loved one through basic meditation alone. Part of the healing process of grief is dealing with spirituality in a way, especially if the person is religious; stones connected to the Crown Chakra are this helpful to mitigate pain from loss.

Inspiration and creativity can be influenced by everything, whether it is from a new art project or a blueprint idea, or if a new way of looking at a problem is needed. Several stones help to boost creativity, namely Carnelian and Citrine. Simply keep the crystal by you while focusing on your project, or meditate with it; either method will help with achieving the spark of inspiration.

While stress is a necessary component to life and achieving goals, relaxation is the balance. Relaxation is the water that's used when tempering the iron, so to speak. Abalone and Turquoise are exceptionally useful stones for helping to manage thoughts and achieve relaxation. Keep one close at hand, meditate with, or sleep with one to receive the effects.

Productivity is what keeps us moving throughout the day, the constant strive to find something to do. Many of us have the ability to work, but aren't forward-thinking enough to know where to start. Thankfully, there are a couple crystals to help; Azurite and Ruby have properties of both boosting energy and encouraging decisiveness. Meditating with these or keeping them close at hand should help your work ethic extensively.

Motivation is both a trait we all require to perform tasks, and an important literary device for finding why someone does something. Finding it is important, though many of us struggle; lack of motivation is also an effect of depression. Stones like Garnet and Tourmaline are extensively useful for helping to find the frame of mind required for performing certain tasks. Sleep with one on your bedside table, or keep one in your pocket to help you.

Focus is an important part of keeping thoughts together, and keeping focused on current events and situations. Lack of focus is caused by a blocked Third Eye Chakra, so any stones associated with that will help for the regaining of concentration in cognitive tasks. Some other examples of helpful stones are Fluorite and Hematite. Simply keep one by you and/or hold it or rub it while you're working to help with achieving the goal.

To quote the Bourne Identity books, "sleep is a weapon." It is a highly underrated tool that is medically required for people to function at peak efficiency (save for a select few), and lack of sleep can affect mood. Moreover, many suffer from insomnia, and are physically unable to sleep. Moonstone and Lepidolite are useful for the ability to detoxify the body of stressful energy keeping you awake, and help to achieve sleep. Keep one by your bed or meditate with one before you go to sleep to achieve the benefits of an easier rest.

MEDITATING WITH CRYSTALS

The term "meditation" has sprung multiple times in the descriptions in these pages, and for good reason. Meditation is the process of calming the mind through causing it to become a blank slate, momentarily. For millennia, it has been a powerful and simple method of thinking clearly and relieving ailments in various different centers of the body, and many different cultures and religions claim meditation to be one of their true tenets. Buddhism, Taoism, and some would even say Catholic Monasticism all practice meditation religiously, though it is not exclusive to them. Meditation is deceptively simple to do, and does not require any specific religious affiliation to work properly.

Meditation is able to be linked to the stones in several various ways, both practically and historically. The Hindu people that have claimed to discover the Chakras and some crystals associated with them have used meditation to clear their minds of negative energy before. However, meditation works by opening the mind and making it blank of all thoughts negative or positive, therefore letting the crystals work much easier with the blank canvas. In this way, meditation works a lot like cleansing a crystal, in that it cleanses the mind of conflicting energies to allow it to be filled with positive ones.

To begin meditation, it is recommended to be in a seated or lying position, preferably on one's back. Relax the muscles, feeling them relieve themselves of tension, and begin breathing evenly and deeply. Your hands should not be doing anything but resting somewhere, and speaking interrupts both the breathing and thinking states.

At the point of relaxing the muscles, begin concentrating only on your breathing. The mind should be focused solely on the inhale and exhale, which should fit a constant, steady, comfortable rhythm. Retain this focus, and try not to think of anything else; this opens the mind to allow the energy of either crystals or another medium to come in. Keep the crystal in close contact with your body, or no more than one foot away for best results.

Meditation serves quite a few purposes. It can allow the body to relax itself, even without the use of a crystal. It can allow the mind to think more clearly and evenly by the act of meditation alone. It can allow for the expulsion of negative energies that attack mood and state of mind, and expel feelings of dread, sadness, or anger. With crystals, this process can become faster or more thorough depending on the crystal and the state of energy the crystal has (or doesn't have).

Crystals can be used to funnel the negative energy into themselves, a recommended purpose would be for someone who is overwhelmed with stress or sadness. They can also allow for the positive energy to be channeled into the body more immediately than carrying it around, since the body is ready to accept new energy. Crystals can also target a specific area of need, such as obtaining clearer communication, better grounding, or a better sense of understanding. In any case, the use of crystals seemingly amplifies the power that meditation can bring forth, if the crystal has been prepared properly.

A few common misconceptions about meditation have been discovered by practitioners to be false. You do not have to keep your hands on your elbows and curl your index finger and thumb into a circle; as long as your hands aren't distracting you, you can keep them wherever you wish. You also do not have to spend hours performing the process; you can be finished in as much as five minutes, if the need isn't dire or you can clear your mind quickly. It is not unknown for people to perform meditation in either of these ways, however, though the person performing is not as limited to these misguided tenets as is traditionally thought.

Make sure that you keep the room you're in free of any distractions or loud noises while you meditate. The point is to lose attention to the distractions that are being thrown your way, and it would be counterproductive to have too many things going on at once. Keep in mind, sometimes mediation has to wait; don't be afraid to get out of the meditative state if something pressing is happening, or simply don't go into meditation at all until the obstacle has been dealt with.

The knowledge of proper form of meditation will allow for better use of crystals, in almost exponential degree. Crystals act in unison with a mind that is willing to accept the energy they have in them. Be warned: make sure the crystal has been cleansed, cleared, and programmed first, as the adverse effect could happen if it has negative charge.

CONCLUSION

With new knowledge coming up about crystals every other day, this book makes an excellent primer on knowledge that already exists. However, this is simply a primer; for more extensive knowledge, there are other books and websites perfect for learning of the history and other properties of these fine stones. New information comes to light every so often, so it's an excellent idea to stay updated on current events when it comes to crystals.

Nevertheless, thank you for buying and reading this book on crystal therapy. You'll be on the fast track to serenity if you apply the knowledge from this book, and more. Surprisingly, many of the sites that attempt to sell crystals are historically correct. Generally speaking, the salesmen get their facts right when it comes to their properties and attributes, although there are always exceptions.

This book is an excellent resource for those just getting into the widespread thesis of crystals, but it is simply an opener. As the author, I encourage you to find out more for yourself, and I don't mean just facts; search for what you want, and what you want to imprint into the crystals, what methods of cleansing and programming work best for you, and whatever little boxes to keep them in you like best.

These crystals can be some of the best things to happen in the lives of many, and serve as a good alternative for many medicines and overcomplicated treatments and therapies. Like almost anything else in the world, you'll end up shaving off some money for these, but if you keep them maintained and safe, you'll likely only have to do it once. Quartz and Amethyst are excellent starting crystals, as they are both hard and thus unlikely to break easily, as well as versatile for many different general ailments and conditions you might have.

Keep them close, keep them safe, and keep them cleansed, and you'll have problems with stress or melancholy much less than you had before using them. Once you discover the properties of these amazing stones, you'll be keeping a piece of Hematite or Aquamarine wherever you go.

Thank you so much from the bottom of my heart for reading.
I wish you the very best life you can possibly imagine.
Please add a short review on Amazon
and let me know what you thought!

Printed in Great Britain
by Amazon